DAVE DRAVECKY

Other Books in the **Today's Heroes** Series

Ben Carson

As a kid his knife was a weapon—now he uses it to save lives.

Joni's Story

When Joni Eareckson learned she'd never walk again, she wanted to die. Little did she know what was in store.

TODAY'S HEROES

DAVE DRAVECKY

by Dave Dravecky
with Tim Stafford

ZondervanPublishingHouse
Grand Rapids, Michigan

A Division of HarperCollinsPublishers

Dave Dravecky
Abridged from the book *Comeback*
Comeback copyright © 1990 by Dave Dravecky
Abridgment copyright © 1992 by Zondervan Publishing House

Requests for information should be addressed to:
Zondervan Publishing House
Grand Rapids, Michigan 49530

Library of Congress Cataloging-in-Publication Data

Dravecky, Dave.
    Dave Dravecky / by Dave Dravecky with Tim Stafford.
       p. cm. — (Today's heroes series)
    Summary: The All-Star pitcher discusses his career in baseball, his battle
with cancer, and his faith in God.
    ISBN 0-310-58651-8 (pbk.)
    1. Dravecky, Dave—Juvenile literature. 2. Baseball players—
United States—Biography—Juvenile literature. 3. Cancer—
Patients—United States—Biography—Juvenile literature.
[1. Dravecky, Dave. 2. Baseball players. 3. Cancer—Patients.
4. —Christian life.] I. Stafford, Tim. II. Title. III. Series.
GV865.D66A3   1992
796.357'092—dc20
[B]   92–16126
                                           CIP
                                         AC

*Published in association with Sealy M. Yates, Literary Agent, Orange,
California.*

Abridged by Tim Stafford
Edited by Lori J. Walburg
Interior designed by Rachel Hostetter
Cover and interior illustrations by Gloria Oostema

Printed in the United States of America

    93 94 95 96 / LP / 10 9 8 7 6 5 4

To Janice

To be blessed with the most precious of all gems is truly a gift from God. You are the wind beneath my wings.

CONTENTS

Chronology of Events

February 14, 1956. Dave Dravecky is born in Boardman, Ohio.

June, 1978. Dravecky graduates from Youngstown State University and is drafted by the Pittsburgh Pirates in the twenty-first round.

October 7, 1987. Dravecky pitches for the San Francisco Giants in the National League championship series against the St. Louis Cardinals and wins 5–0.

January 26, 1988. Tests indicate that a lump on Dravecky's left arm is probably benign.

April 4, 1988. Dravecky pitches opening day against the Los Angeles Dodgers, winning 5–1.

June 11, 1988. Surgery on Dravecky's left shoulder puts him on the disabled list for the rest of the 1988 season.

September 19, 1988. Dr. Muschler indicates that Dravecky's lump may be cancerous.

October 7, 1988. Surgery removes one-half of the deltoid muscle in Dravecky's pitching arm.

January 9, 1989. Doctors give the okay for throwing a football and plan a rehabilitation schedule that could bring Dravecky back to pitch by midsummer.

July 8, 1989. In St. Louis, Dravecky pitches his first simulated game.

July 23, 1989. Dravecky pitches for the Class-A San Jose Giants in Stockton, California, before 4,200 fans. He pitches a complete game and wins 2–0.

August 4, 1989. Moving to Triple-A Phoenix, Dravecky leads the Firebirds over Tucson, 3–2, in a complete-game seven-hitter.

August 10, 1989. Dravecky pitches his first major league game in over a year, going for eight innings against the Cincinnati Reds and winning 4–3.

August 15, 1989. While pitching in Montreal, Dravecky's arm breaks.

October 9, 1989. While celebrating victory in the National League championship series, Dravecky's arm is broken again.

October 17, 1989. An earthquake stops the World Series.

October 27, 1989. Doctors at the Cleveland Clinic tell Dravecky that cancer has probably recurred in his arm.

November 13, 1989. Dravecky announces his retirement from baseball.

June 18, 1991. Dravecky's left arm and shoulder are amputated.

1

Between the Lines

When I was a kid, I dreamed of playing baseball in the major leagues. My love for the game started with neighborhood games right in my own backyard, in Youngstown, Ohio. I always loved to play. I loved to pitch. I loved the challenge of getting a batter out with a blazing fastball.

When I got a little older I played Little League, and my dad was the coach. I still remember some of those games: who we played, the name of the opposing pitcher, the score. One game, I was pitching against Mike Berezo of the Bears Club. It was a classic pitchers' duel. I threw a no-hitter, and we won 1–0.

I used to imitate Sandy Koufax, one of the

greatest pitchers of all time, and a lefty like me. That's how I got a high leg kick—Koufax had one. I wanted to be a pitcher in the major leagues, just like Sandy Koufax.

You know what? The dream came true. In high school and college, my three brothers quit playing baseball, and so did a lot of my friends, but I kept on. Out of college I got drafted into professional ball in the twenty-first round—one of the last picks in the draft. It meant the scouts weren't expecting too much from me.

I played five years in the minor leagues, but I wasn't ever considered a hot prospect. In fact, some coaches told me I didn't have the talent for the major leagues. But I was determined. I never lost my dream. And finally it came true. One day I was called up to the big leagues, to play for the San Diego Padres. Working mostly as a relief pitcher, I made the All-Star team, and I pitched in the play-offs and in the World Series.

For any kid who loves baseball, that's a dream come true. I never thought anything could top it. This book, though, is about something that went beyond my dreams. This book is about an amazing year in baseball—a gift God gave me that I will never forget. It is about the year I came back from cancer.

*   *   *

Dave Dravecky

I first noticed the lump in the fall of 1987. A firm, round shape about the size of a quarter was under the skin on my left arm. I asked our trainer about it, but he didn't think I should worry. It didn't hurt. So I didn't pay attention to it. I had other things on my mind.

I was thinking about the National League championship series. For the second time in my baseball career, I was playing in the postseason. This time I was a starting pitcher for the San Francisco Giants. We had won our division and were getting ready to take on the St. Louis Cardinals in the play-offs.

I started the second game in St. Louis. It was a night game, cold as October can be. Overhead, above the lights, the sky was utterly black.

We had lost the first game by a score of 5–3. To win the play-offs and go on to the World Series, we had to win the second game. I would be opposing John Tudor, an outstanding pitcher.

I wasn't nervous. Excited, yes. As soon as I got on the mound and threw my first pitch, I became totally absorbed by the game. I saw my catcher, Bob Melvin. I saw his glove. I didn't see much else. I was in the groove.

In the top of the second inning, Candy Maldonado, our right fielder, led off with a crisp single. He was followed by Will Clark, who locked on a pitch and with a long, smooth, effortless swing of his bat sent it high in the air to right field. José Oquendo backed up to the fence, as though he had a bead on it. But the ball fell into the stands for a home run. Suddenly, with hardly any warning, we were ahead 2–0. Busch Stadium fell absolutely quiet.

And I kept it quiet. I was pitching the game of my life. Every time the 55,331 fans stirred to life, I quieted them. It was an incredible feeling of power.

In the fourth inning, our left fielder Jeffrey Leonard came to the plate. The Cardinal fans had taken a dislike to Jeffrey. They taunted him: "Jeff-REE! Jeff-REE!"

Leonard is a strong, proud, tough-looking dude. He fouled off a few pitches and then went deep to straightaway center field. The ball seemed to take a long time to settle over the fence for a home run, and Leonard took even longer to circle the bases. It was 3–0. Busch Stadium was silent again.

I was locked in. Fifty thousand fans did not exist to me. Even the batters barely existed. Only my catcher was there. He knew what I wanted to throw. I knew that he knew. Some of the time we didn't even use signs.

In the top of the fifth inning, we almost broke it open. I even got a hit. But we blew a squeeze play and didn't score. The fans began to buzz. The momentum seemed to shift. The Cardinals were coming to life.

Dave Dravecky

I went out to the mound thinking, "Keep on cheering. Make a little more noise. Because the silence will be that much greater when we're done with this inning."

I was stoked. Not that you'd know it by looking at me. My confidence doesn't come through in my face. I keep the fire out of my eyes so my opponents don't see what I'm feeling.

But I felt confident to my bones. I went out there with the crowd stirring and beginning to chant, and I put them back to sleep.

We scored twice more in the eighth inning, thanks to a very rare error by Ozzie Smith. With a five-run lead I coasted home with my first postseason win. I'd given up two hits and no runs, putting myself in the record books. In the 1984 play-offs and World Series I'd pitched five times in relief and not given up a run. Now I'd run my postseason record to nineteen and two-thirds scoreless innings.

After the game I was summoned to the interview room. Roger Craig was talking to a room jammed full of reporters. I could barely get through the crush.

Someone asked Roger a question about Christian ballplayers—something about Christians being too nice to be winners.

Roger said, "They say Christians don't have any guts. Well, this guy's a Christian and he's not

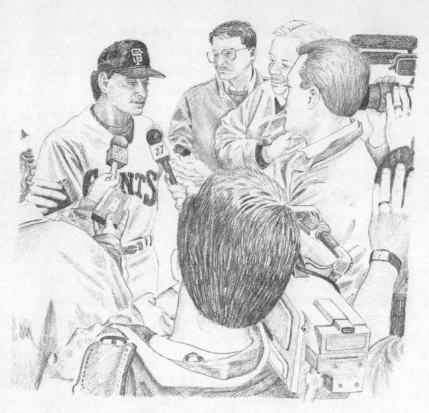

afraid of anything." He handed the microphone over to me.

Right away a writer asked me, "How do you respond to that?"

They were asking me whether Christians are wimps. The best way to answer that question, I thought, was to ask whether Jesus was a wimp. After all, Christians are followers of Jesus.

I told them that if Jesus were in my shoes,

Dave Dravecky

called to compete as a professional athlete, he would be the best athlete on the field. He would play with more intensity and aggressiveness than any other athlete. But he would always be under control.

I said to the reporters, "Jesus Christ is my example. I play for him. When I play, I play to glorify God. I recognize the ability he's given me, and so I play with everything I have."

I loved getting the chance to tell them that.

My wife, Janice, met me as I came out of the clubhouse. That day was the ninth anniversary of our wedding. I'd pitched a shutout in the play-offs. I'd had a chance to give credit where credit is due—to God.

Looking at me with stars in her eyes, Janice said, "I don't know how you're going to top this."

2

Is This My Year?

What *could* top that? If I'd stopped to think seriously about it, I might have thought of starting in the World Series. But that wasn't going to happen.

We went home to Candlestick Park and won two out of the next three games. When we returned to St. Louis, we needed to win just one of the last two. I started the first game; my best friend, Atlee Hammaker, was to pitch the second, if necessary.

As Atlee and I came into the ballpark, he kept telling me, "You've got to win this one for us, Dave. You've got to win."

"Hey, it's no big deal, Atlee," I said. "If I don't win today, you'll win tomorrow."

I did my best. My pitching, in fact, was better

than in my first play-off game. I didn't walk a man, and I struck out eight in six innings. The damage was done by one of those little things.

In the second inning, Cardinal catcher Tony Pena led off with a weak line drive to right field. But Candy hesitated, made a feet-first slide—and missed the ball completely. By the time Chili Davis ran it down from his center field position, Pena had coasted into third.

Candy had lost the ball in the lights. At that point, in the second inning, it didn't seem like such a big deal. I got Willie McGee to hit into a ground out, and Pena—who isn't terribly speedy—had to hold at third. José Oquendo came up. He hit a shallow fly ball down the right field line, which Maldonado raced for and caught. Candy had to turn his body halfway around to throw. Maybe he tried a little too hard. The ball bounced off-line on the third-base side, and Pena scored what turned out to be the only run of the game. John Tudor pitched brilliantly against us. We lost 1–0.

The next night Atlee went out and got hit hard. For the second night in a row our team couldn't score a single run. And before we knew it we were on our way home to lick our wounds and watch the other guys play the World Series.

Losing to the Cardinals was tough, but I remembered all the good times. Our team had done extremely well, and I had pitched the best

games of my life in the most important games of my life.

During that off-season I got the lump on my arm checked. The doctors did an MRI (Magnetic Resonance Image), which makes you feel like an experiment done in a science fiction movie. The doctors strap you down to a small table. Then with a low rumble the table slides you into a large metal

Dave Dravecky

cylinder, about the length and width of a human body.

I was in the cylinder for two hours. While inside I had to lie absolutely still, strapped down, looking up at the top of the cylinder a few inches above my nose. All I could think about was what I would do in case of an earthquake. How would I get out of there?

The results showed I'd been right not to feel concern. The doctors told me to keep an eye on the lump and have it examined again in six months.

*　*　*

I launched the '88 season in Dodger Stadium, going up against the great Fernando Valenzuela. The stadium was jammed, the weather perfect. We Giants were psyched up for the season. We fully expected to win our division again, and this time to go on to the World Series.

I'll never forget my first pitch. I threw a fast ball down and in to Steve Sax. He pulled out and jerked it down the line. The ball flew out of the park like a bullet. The crowd went into a frenzy.

It wasn't a very good beginning to a new season. I thought to myself, "Oh, no. Here we go!" But then I said, "Okay, forget it. You can't change it. Let's go on from here."

Is This My Year?   23

I proceeded to shut the Dodgers out on three hits the rest of the way. I had the feeling, that delicious sense of absolute control. We won 5–1.

You have dreams and you set goals. For all pitchers, the dream is a twenty-game winning season. This year, I thought, I'll do it. I even told my wife, Janice, when I got home to San Francisco. "You know something, baby? I think 1988 is going to be my year."

3

Tumor

It didn't work out that way. From that glorious opening day I took a ride on a roller coaster. One moment I was on top, winning games. The next I was hurtling down, wondering if anything could ever stop my fall.

The trouble was, my shoulder hurt. Whenever I tried to throw hard, it would kill me. I got very frustrated. To get beat by a batter was one thing, but to get beat by a sore shoulder was another. Finally, in May, I was put on the disabled list. Eventually I had surgery.

While I was recuperating, Atlee and I hung around a lot together. Atlee was on me about the lump on my arm. "Man, that lump is getting bigger!" he'd say. He wanted me to see another doctor. But I wasn't thinking about it. I was much more concerned about my shoulder.

Despite the operation, my shoulder still hurt, and I wasn't able to pitch. The team wasn't doing well either. Finally, near the end of the season, I asked if I could just go home to Ohio. The Giants said I could.

By then the lump on my arm was clearly visible—big as a golf ball, and as hard as one, too. Six months had gone by since my last exam. It was time to get the lump checked again. So just before leaving San Francisco, I went for another MRI. A few days later the doctor called me in Ohio and said I'd better see a doctor near my home.

So Janice and I drove up to Cleveland for an appointment. Neither of us was very worried. We thought this was just a routine check on a minor problem.

We were sitting in a small examining room, talking quietly together, when we heard people shuffling around outside the door. Apparently Dr. Bergfeld had arrived. He was looking at the film from my MRI, we knew, because we heard the film flap into position over the lights. Then we heard four distinct words from one deep voice: "Look at that tumor."

"Tumor." No one had ever used that word before. They had talked about a lump, not a tumor.

Tumor was a scary word. Hearing it, we felt as though the entire floor fell away.

I looked at Janice. She looked at me. I could see from her eyes that she was shocked and scared. "I think we better pray," she said.

"Yeah," I said. "We better pray right now."

I got off the examining table and sat on a chair beside her. We held hands.

"Dear God," I said, "we don't know what's happening. We don't know what this means. Help us to face whatever comes."

Then Dr. Bergfeld came in.

*   *   *

I felt at home with Dr. Bergfeld right away. I can't think of anybody I'd rather meet just moments after hearing the word "tumor." He is a big man, with a hearty, booming voice and a jolly manner. He has a way of making you feel that everything is in good hands. He told me right away, "Dave, this may be a tumor. I'm going to send you up to see an oncologist."

When he said "oncologist," my heart skipped a beat. I knew that an oncologist is a cancer doctor.

So we went to see Dr. Muschler. He said, "I recommend you have a biopsy on this. I don't think we're dealing with a high grade malignant tumor. But we can't be sure."

I wanted to scream, "What do you mean you can't be sure? You're talking about my life!"

He thought it was a kind of tumor that wouldn't spread to other parts of my body. If so, it wasn't deadly. "But we need to take a biopsy and find out."

A biopsy is when the doctor cuts off a tiny piece of your tumor so they can test it. It didn't take long, maybe half an hour, and it didn't hurt.

Afterwards, Dr. Muschler talked to us again. He seemed optimistic. He drew a picture to show us where the tumor was growing on my deltoid muscle. The deltoid is the large muscle that wraps over the top of your shoulder. Dr. Muschler said the tumor was near where the muscle attaches to the large bone of my upper arm, the humerus bone. He was reasonably certain that it wasn't a deadly kind of tumor. "But I can't be one hundred percent sure," he said.

The days following the biopsy were quiet ones. The baseball season had ended and the play-offs were about to begin, but I was living in a world far away from that. Baseball didn't matter much now that my life was in danger.

I didn't have much to say. I sat quietly and filled my eyes with my wife and my children. I couldn't get enough of being near them.

It was an anxious time, waiting, just waiting to

Dave Dravecky

hear the news. When the phone rang I always wondered whether I would hear the results.

Yet it was a good kind of anxiety, too. Just looking at Janice reminded me how much I loved her. I stared at her and I stared at my kids, thinking they were the most beautiful sight in the entire universe. Some nights when Tiffany and Jonathan were asleep I would go into their room and listen to them slowly breathing. I thought of how often I didn't have time for them. Many times when they had asked me to play ball, I'd told them, "I'm busy reading right now; give me ten minutes"—and then the phone would ring and I never would get to play with them. During those days of waiting I did play ball, or whatever else they wanted to play.

I also thought about where I would go when I died. I knew God would welcome me to heaven. That meant a lot to me.

One thought did not enter my mind. I never thought, "Why me?" I didn't feel sorry for myself. I wasn't wondering why God had treated me so unfairly.

I know that those thoughts do come to people who face cancer, because many people have asked me about them. I don't claim any credit for myself, but I didn't have those thoughts. Janice didn't either. We just didn't think that way. To explain why, I'd have to take you back to my days as a minor league baseball player.

4

Lessons from Amarillo

I was playing minor league baseball in Amarillo, Texas, when I met a guy named Byron Ballard. He had brilliant red hair and freckles; he was tall, with size fifteen feet. I liked him right away. Everybody did. He seemed incredibly joyful about life and had a wonderful, zany sense of humor.

The first time I met him I saw some Christian books on his bed, and I commented on it. I grew up in a religious home, and I always had a respect for God. In times of trouble, I prayed. I went to church on Sunday when I could.

From my comments, Byron thought I was a

Dave Dravecky

born-again Christian. I saw his eyes light up, thinking that he had found a fellow believer. So I had to straighten him out. "I'm sorry," I said, "but there's no way. I really don't understand that born-again stuff at all."

I suppose most people would have quit there, but Byron didn't. He kept talking to me. He tried to explain what "born again" meant. More than that, he got out a Bible and showed me where Jesus talked about it. (It's in John 3:3.) I was impressed. The guy obviously knew something.

During the next weeks, we talked again and again. Byron was not ramming anything down my throat. On the contrary, I was asking him questions. During the past two years, Janice and I had been through some terribly tough times while I played winter ball in Colombia. For the first time in my life, I'd found myself crying out to God for help.

I already knew that there was a God, I considered myself a Christian, and I believed that the Bible was God's Word. But I really didn't know how to relate to God. To me, God was distant and impersonal. You respected him, but you didn't really know him. I had never read the Bible. Once, when we were first married, Janice had suggested we read it together. But I said no way. "I can never read that thing, Janice. It doesn't even make sense. It's for the priests to read, not me."

I soon found out, through Byron, that the Bible

contained plenty of things I could understand. I started reading it for myself, and it turned my ideas upside down about God. God wasn't distant and vague. In the Bible, he was active and close to people. In fact, he had come to earth as Jesus and had died for people like me.

I had a lot of questions. I felt I was basically a good person. I didn't understand why Byron thought I was a sinner. I knew that I wasn't perfect, but did that make me a sinner?

Byron showed me where the Bible says that all human beings are sinners, because all fall short of the glory God intended them to have. (That's in Romans 3:23.) I was amazed. I couldn't understand why no one had told me this before.

My next question was: How do I get rid of my sin and begin to relate to God? Byron again showed me places in the Bible that showed me how to confess my sins and ask God to forgive me. One of these Bible verses, Romans 10:9, became my theme: "If you confess with your mouth, 'Jesus is Lord,' and believe in your heart that God raised him from the dead, you will be saved."

I didn't become a believer overnight. I watched Byron like a hawk, trying to figure him out. It wasn't what he said that convinced me so much as the way he lived. In every situation he was full of joy, brimming over with love for God.

When Janice came to Amarillo, she was afraid I

Dave Dravecky

was turning into a religious nut. But with the help of other people and a few books she began sorting through her own questions. Gradually she also grew excited about God.

We could see that if God was as personal as Byron—and the Bible—said, our life would have to change. If God truly cared about every detail of life, we couldn't assume that we knew what was best for ourselves.

Eventually we made a decision. We committed ourselves to follow the personal God we learned about in the Bible, to follow Jesus wherever he might lead us.

Ever since then, in good times and hard times, we've known that God cared for us. That lesson, learned in Amarillo, helped us deal with the news we heard seven years later at the Cleveland Clinic.

It prevented us from getting bitter and angry about the tumor. Life isn't always fair, but the Bible taught me not to confuse life with God. When bad things happen to you, you don't ask, "Why me?" You ask God, "What do you want me to do in this situation?"

I entered this difficult time trusting that God was for me. Jesus had given his life for Janice and me. There was nothing else—no other good thing—he would keep back. That belief gave us hope to face what would come.

Lessons from Amarillo

* * *

A week after the biopsy we discussed the results with Dr. Muschler. He explained that I had a desmoid tumor. Just as he'd thought, it wasn't a deadly kind of cancer. But we needed to take action. "If you leave one single cell in there, it can grow into another tumor. We have to cut it out with a wide margin all around. I'm afraid we'll have to take out at least half of your deltoid muscle."

"What about my career?" I said. "Tell it to me straight, Doc. I'm not afraid."

Dr. Muschler thought for a moment and then spoke quietly. "Well, Dave, if you have this operation I think your chances of returning to professional baseball are zero."

When he said "professional" I thought I heard "major leagues."

"That's okay, Dr. Muschler," I said. "I don't mind pitching minor league ball and working my way back up. Even if it takes a couple of years, that's all right."

Dr. Muschler interrupted. "Dave, I don't think you understood me." He spoke firmly. "Losing half your deltoid muscle will take away one of the three most powerful muscles in your arm. My greatest hope is that you will someday play catch with your son in your backyard."

Dave Dravecky

The room was very quiet. "You mean, no professional ball at all?" I said.

He said no.

"So what do you want to do, Dave?" he asked me.

I did not hesitate. "Hey, Doc, if that's the way it is, let's get on with it. Don't think I'm going to go off in a little closet and cry. I've had a great career, I've enjoyed every minute of it, and I'm ready to go on with whatever is next."

That's what I said and what I felt. I'd been in an All-Star game. I'd pitched in two National League championships and one World Series. I'd had a taste of every good thing baseball had to offer. What did I have to cry about?

I told him, "If I never play again, Doc, I'll know that God has someplace else he wants me. But I'll tell you something else. I believe in a God who can do miracles. If you remove half my deltoid muscle, that doesn't mean I'll never pitch again. If God wants me to pitch, it doesn't matter whether you remove all of the deltoid muscle. If God wants me to pitch, I'll be out there."

Dr. Muschler just looked at me. He must have thought I was a little crazy.

We set the date for surgery at October 7—one year to the day after I'd won the second game of the National League championships for the Giants.

5

Under the Knife

I felt full of high spirits as the nurses rolled me down to the operating room. I told them, "I just want you guys to know one thing before you put me under. A lot of people back home are praying for you right now. God's in control of this thing and I've got all the confidence in the world in every one of you. So have fun!"

One of them told me it was the first time a patient had said that people were praying for *them*. But who better to pray for? They were going to be doing the work! I was just going to be lying on my side for the rest of the day.

It wasn't quite that easy, though. I was in the operating room for thirteen hours. I woke up in

blinding pain. For the first day after the operation I felt awful.

The operation, Dr. Muschler said, had gone well. He had cut around both sides of the tumor, clear to the bone. Then he cut my deltoid muscle in two, and it became like a broken rubber band. I would have to learn to live without a deltoid muscle.

The most difficult part of the surgery was separating the tumor from the bone. Dr. Muschler used a little hand spray gun, filled with liquid nitrogen. He and his assistants sprayed the muscle where it attached to the bone. A line of frost quickly developed. They waited until it thawed out—that took fifteen minutes—then froze it again. After a second thawing, it was frozen a third time. Then they peeled the muscle off the bone and began spraying another line. The freezing and thawing was killing the tumor where it was attached to the bone, but it was also killing the cells of the bone. For the next six months, my arm would be very brittle, easy to break. Eventually, though, it would heal itself.

After he had frozen the tumor, Dr. Muschler lifted it gently out of my arm and handed it to one of his assistants. I wish I could have seen it. I wish that I had asked Dr. Muschler to keep the tumor for me in a jar, so I could have seen the alien that was cut out of my body.

* * *

After five days in the hospital I came home to live in my parents' basement—what Janice and I called the dungeon. There at the bottom of steep stairs is one of the most uncomfortable fold-out couches in America. We slept on its lumps and ridges for slightly over a month, while our new house was being built.

I should say we *tried* to sleep. Normally, I thrash around and destroy my bed every night. Now I had to lie flat on my back. If I rolled to one side or the other the pain was unbearable. Sleeping flat on my back meant that I didn't sleep. I dozed fitfully. I lay awake squirming, wondering whether a comfortable position existed.

Those weeks were difficult for me. I was constantly in pain, I couldn't get a good night's sleep, and I was facing the end of my baseball career. I wasn't bitter, but I was sad.

A few nights after getting home I watched the Dodgers play the fifth and final game of the World Series, finishing off the A's. It wasn't a very close game. With Orel Hershiser on the mound, it was obvious the A's hitters were overmastered.

Janice went to bed, but I remained upstairs. The sofa felt as comfortable as my bed in the basement, so I thought I might as well stay put. The room was dark except for the dim light from the TV.

I saw Orel make the last pitch of the game, striking out Tony Phillips. I saw him throw a quick glance to heaven, thanking God. I saw him engulfed in the surging mass of Dodger blue.

I was happy, because I had been rooting for the Dodgers. I was truly happy for Orel, knowing that he shares my faith in Christ and that he is a great guy. Yet I couldn't help thinking how the season had begun for me against the Dodgers. I had been the dominant pitcher. It had looked like my year. It could have been me on that mound.

Instead, it appeared that I was done with baseball. A week before I had been healthy and strong. Now I was pitiful.

I never cry. Sometimes I wish I could shed tears, to express my feelings more freely, but I am not someone who can. That night, though, I cried. All alone, in the dark, I broke into big, fat tears.

*   *   *

You always wonder how it will be to go through a difficult time. You talk about the love of God, yet you can't help wondering: *When tough times come will I really be able to live it?*

Janice and I found that we could. We found that faith carried us through our troubles, day by day. We felt God's love, not ending our troubles, but strengthening us to deal with them.

The first Sunday after getting out of the hospital we went to church. We purposely arrived a bit late, so I would not have to greet too many people as I hobbled painfully in. We found a seat in the very back. People sneaked a peek at me and quickly looked away. I was a sorry sight, limping slowly with a cane, my arm in a sling. My face told the story of the battle I was in.

In our church we sometimes have a time when anybody can stand up and share what's happening to them—either thanking God, or asking for prayer. I hadn't planned on participating, but when others began sharing, I made up my mind I had something to say. I rose slowly to my feet, balancing with my cane.

"I want to praise God for your prayers." I spoke very slowly, because as soon as I got up my emotions flooded over me. "I want you to know how much it meant, that people here were praying for me."

My voice began to crack, then suddenly I began to cry. "During the whole week at the hospital," I said, "I had a tremendous sense of peace. I felt the presence of God with me. I knew that my faith and your prayers made a difference.

"I've come to the place," I said, "where if I never play baseball again it's okay with me."

6

Comeback?

The doctor said my baseball career was through, and I believed him. I knew God could do miracles, but I wasn't at all sure he would do one in my case. I didn't beg him for one. I had enjoyed a wonderful life in baseball, and if God wanted me to go on to something else, I wasn't going to argue with him. My part was to cooperate with the doctors and do all I could to recover from surgery.

That meant physical therapy. Without a deltoid muscle, I had lost certain kinds of motion. For example, the doctor told me that it would be really hard for me to reach behind me to my hip pocket and take out my wallet. Through physical therapy I could retrain my shoulder to use other muscles.

Dave Dravecky

I worked hard with my physical therapist. The workouts were very tiring, and often they seemed pointless. Sometimes I really didn't feel like going.

Day by day, though, I made progress. One day about five weeks after surgery, I came home from my therapy workout and found Janice washing the dishes.

"Hey, I've got something to show you," I said. "Watch this."

Using my left arm, I slowly reached behind me to my rear pants pocket. I took out my wallet and set it down on the counter.

"Oh, wow!" Janice hopped up and down with excitement. Dr. Muschler had said I'd need months of rehabilitation before I could take the wallet out of my pocket.

"That's not all," I said. "Watch this."

I stepped up into the kitchen area, where she could see me clearly. Then slowly and deliberately, I went through my pitching motion. It felt the way it always had—slower and sorer, but essentially the same.

Janice stared, tears springing into her eyes. We hugged each other. "I can't believe it," she said.

That was the day we really began to hope I would pitch again.

Pitch? Just a few weeks before the idea had seemed ridiculous. When the Giants called asking

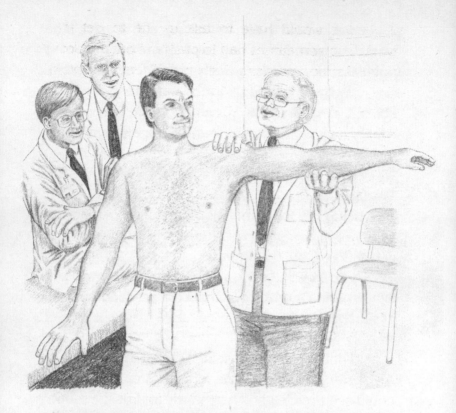

about my plans for spring training, Janice had been annoyed. "Why can't they just leave you alone?"

But after that day, we began to get excited. Was it possible I could come back?

Realistically, though, we were getting ahead of ourselves. I had removed my wallet from my back pocket. That was different from pitching major league baseball.

Sometimes I seemed to make no progress at

Dave Dravecky

all. Janice would have to talk to me to get me going. She sometimes had to push me out the door to my therapy sessions. I always felt much better when I came home after a workout, though, knowing I'd done what I could.

I knew that the odds were against my coming back. My part, I believed, was to do everything possible, to try with all my might. Then, if I couldn't pitch, God would have other, better things for me to do. Trust in God helped me to work hard and not to worry about the outcome.

*   *   *

On January 9, a Monday, I was scheduled to meet with the doctors at the Cleveland Clinic. I looked forward to amazing them.

"Okay, Dave," one of the doctors said, "go through the motions for us. Show us what you can do."

First I performed the movements I knew wouldn't surprise them, like reaching over my head. Then I worked into the motions that I knew would blow them away, like starting with my hand at my side and pushing it straight back, or starting with my hand at my side and lifting it straight out from my body.

Comeback?   45

I got the response I was looking for. "Wow, Dave, that's good. That's pretty impressive."

But the fun really began after Dr. Muschler came in. He didn't say anything until I began pushing my arm straight back from a position at my side.

Muschler said, "How are you doing that?" He came up to me and put his hands on my shoulder. "Do it, Dave." So I did it. "Do it again." He was feeling my muscles work, trying to understand what was moving my arm. In a low, thinking-to-himself voice, he said, "You must be using your lats." Then he stepped back and stared at me, as though he were looking for a trick. He took a chair in the corner of the room, and from then on just sat there, not talking unless someone asked him a question.

Dr. Bergfeld came in. "Well, Dave, how are you doing?" he asked in his booming voice. I said I was doing great, and began going through the motions. He started crowing. "You see?" he said to Muschler. "You see? I told you that you weren't dealing with an ordinary individual here. He's an athlete, and they're different."

Dr. Muschler just sat in his corner, saying, "I'm really impressed."

We all talked at once, celebrating together. Then came a pause. Bergfeld looked at Muschler. "Well," he boomed, "let's get him throwing! What do you think, George? Can he throw?"

Dave Dravecky

Throw? All these months I had not so much as picked up a baseball. Never once had I cradled that little white ball in my hand. Dr. Muschler had warned me against throwing anything. I hadn't picked up a rock and thrown it against a tree, I hadn't tossed a piece of paper into the waste basket. I'd done my workouts with my little wrist weights. Throw? Throw!

Muschler, however, was quite cautious. The humerus bone, he said, was very brittle because of the freezing he'd done to kill the cancer cells. Generally it took four to six months for someone's bone strength to come back. But my case wasn't "general." Nobody had ever tried to throw baseballs ninety miles an hour after having his bone frozen. Nor had anyone ever tried to do it with half a deltoid muscle.

"So no spring training?" Dr. Bergfeld said. "You don't think he could go down there and take light workouts?"

Muschler thought if I got with all my teammates at spring training, I'd be tempted to say, "Forget those doctors," and let it rip. He was right, too.

"Well, maybe he can go for the last week," Muschler said. "But I don't want him to interrupt his therapy."

I just watched and listened as these two great doctors went back and forth over my treatment.

Whatever they came up with, I was charged up. For the first time the doctors were talking as though baseball was a possibility.

They finally decided to let me start throwing a football. They felt that would be less likely to overstress my arm.

Dr. Muschler gave me a stern warning, though, to pay attention to the way my arm felt. "Any little ache you feel could be a hairline fracture. If you feel the slightest pain you need to quit immediately. If it's a hairline fracture, it'll set you back six weeks. But if it breaks, it sets you back a full year."

When we'd gone over the details of my training program, Dr. Bergfeld asked Dr. Muschler the big question. "Doctor, if everything goes well and Dave follows this program, when do you think he might be at full strength and ready for competition?"

Dr. Muschler's answer surprised me. "Sometime in July," he said, "if everything goes well."

I left the Cleveland Clinic with enough excitement to pitch the World Series.

7

Hitting the Wall

I was so anxious to start playing baseball that I went to Arizona for the last two days of spring training. I was just happy to put on spikes and walk onto a baseball diamond. I found Atlee, played a little catch, and did some running under the blue Arizona sky. Everybody who saw me throw was amazed.

I felt great. For the first time in a year I had no pain in my arm. I told everybody who would listen that I was coming back. I told them I would pitch before the summer was over.

It felt even better to arrive in San Francisco and walk into the clubhouse at Candlestick Park, the Giants' stadium. The guys made me feel welcome immediately. Left fielder Kevin Mitchell examined my arm and said, "Man, you look like Jaws took a bite out of you." Mike Krukow, a pitcher, looked over my body and summed it up: "You're certainly no day at the beach." That's the way ballplayers show their affection. In about sixty seconds I felt like I'd never been gone.

I felt like a living miracle. The thought occurred to me: I've had a year and a half of nearly total rest. Maybe my pitching career will be given an extended life.

* * *

The next day I drove down to see Larry Brown, the Giants' physical therapist. To test my strength, he put me through a series of arm exercises. In some areas he found I had no strength at all. After the workout Larry said that we had a rough road ahead—even rougher than he'd expected. Unlike the others, he didn't seem impressed by what I'd accomplished.

The next morning we began going through arm exercises, just as we had the day before. Just as before, I couldn't do them.

"Let's let it go at that," Larry said in a leaden voice. "There's no use in pushing it beyond what you can do. Let's just go out and throw and see how that feels."

From what he had seen of my arm, Larry couldn't have been expecting much. He probably thought I'd shot-put the ball to him. We got our gloves and went out into the parking lot. I hadn't thrown three times before Larry stopped.

"How are you doing that?" he asked. His tone was completely changed. "You shouldn't be able to throw that way."

It wasn't how hard I was throwing, it was the fact that my delivery was unchanged. Since I was missing most of a major arm muscle, he'd assumed that my delivery would be totally different.

I walked over to him, my glove under my arm. "Larry, I think you understand where I'm coming from. As far as I'm concerned, this has all been a miracle of God."

With that puzzled look on his face, Larry said, "There's no other way to explain it." We went back to throwing.

When we were done Larry seemed much more confident. "All right, let's go," he said. "Let's just get you strong and see where that takes us."

* * *

Every morning, starting about nine o'clock, I worked with Larry. It was a tough day's work.

Oftentimes others who were getting therapy would stop by and look at what we were doing. I can remember them commenting, "Boy, I'm glad you're not working like that on me, Larry."

I'd get home absolutely exhausted. For at least an hour I'd sink into my chair and say nothing. If anybody disturbed me I'd be extremely grumpy.

By the end of April I was beginning to worry. I told Janice, "I'm not getting anywhere. I'm on a plateau."

My arm had gained strength, my stamina had greatly increased, but I still couldn't throw the ball well. I felt as though my arm were dead. There was no snap to it, no vitality. I tried to fire the ball, but I found nothing there.

Larry wasn't too encouraging. He simply pointed out that I was missing a major arm muscle. Maybe I was feeling the medical fact: There *was* nothing there.

After two weeks of frustration, my arm began to hurt. I'd make a few pitches and feel the pain build. Larry gave me a couple of days off, to see whether that would help, but when I tried to throw again the pain was terrible.

Strength wasn't the problem. I was bench pressing more weight than I had in my whole life. The problem was that I couldn't throw. Instead of the cheery, encouraging comments I'd been hearing from my teammates, I began to get a lot of sad looks. Larry drove up to watch me at the ballpark a couple of times. The first time, things went fairly well. The next time, my shoulder felt as though somebody had hammered a nail into it. I had to quit.

Two days later, I went into the outfield to shag balls and throw them back into the infield—just lazy, easy tosses. But my shoulder hurt too much to bear. The ball would loop eighty feet or so and bury itself in the grass. I simply could not throw.

That evening I met with Dr. Campbell, and he recommended that I shut down my workouts completely. He suggested no exercises, no nothing for a month. Only time would tell whether I could ever throw again.

I was in a fog emotionally. Teammates were feeling sorry for me, and I was feeling sorry for myself. I went up to Atlee one day and said, "If I have to retire, Atlee, will you still be my friend?"

"What are you talking about retirement for?" Atlee said. "You're not ready for that."

Janice thought I was, though. One day she took a call from the athletic director of a midwestern college. He said he was interested in discussing a coaching job with me. To Janice, that sounded perfect. We had often talked about how much I'd like coaching at a college level. This way, I could retire and go on to a solid job. She wrote down the number and told me about it when I came home.

I didn't say much. I put the number aside and said I'd call, but I didn't. I wasn't sure why. I just knew I wasn't ready.

Janice reminded me that I was to call back. I put her off. The next day she reminded me again, and I put her off again.

The third day she said, "David, I really don't understand why you're not calling him. Why don't you at least talk to the man?"

Then, suddenly, I knew how I felt. I looked at her. "Don't count me out yet," I said.

All winter, when I'd been gaining strength day by day, I'd told people that I'd use every last ounce of energy to try to make a comeback. Then, if I'd done everything possible and I was truly unable to play, I could accept the end of my baseball career with grace.

I didn't believe I'd reached that point yet. I hadn't used every last ounce of energy. I wasn't done trying.

Dave Dravecky

8

Air It Out

For a month I did nothing but pedal the stationary bike. I showed up at practice, I went to the games, I put on a uniform—but I didn't feel as though I were a real baseball player. I felt like a ghost.

The team was doing well, staying at the top of their division. They played some incredible cliff-hanging games. They lost some dreadfully, and they won some stunningly. Watching the Giants must have been hard on people with heart problems.

All this meant that the Giants weren't spending a lot of time thinking about Dave Dravecky. When you're hurt and the team's doing poorly, people tend to say, "If only you were healthy." But when you're hurt and the team is in first place, people tend to forget you.

The first time I threw after my month of rest, I worked carefully, feeling for the pain in the back of my shoulder. There was some soreness. I took a day off and threw again. This time the pain was unmistakable. I went home in a gloom. "It's back," I told Janice softly. "My shoulder is hurting again. I don't think I'm going to be able to throw."

The next day I told Atlee that my arm was hurting, that I couldn't throw. We were out in right field, shagging fly balls under the afternoon sun. Atlee wouldn't accept what I said. He said, "Come on, Dave. Let's play some catch."

"I don't know, Atlee. I think I'd better not."

"Hey," Atlee replied. "What have you got to lose? You've done your therapy. Your arm is strong. David, the time has come. Don't baby it any more. Let it rip. If it goes, it goes."

He insisted, and I let him talk me into it. We started throwing the ball back and forth. I threw carefully, cautiously, and my shoulder felt okay. The longer I threw, the better I felt.

I told Atlee that it was feeling pretty good.

"All right," he said. "Let's throw through some of that pain. Just work through it. Let's air this baby out."

He backed up and we began to throw hard.

Dave Dravecky

The ball went zipping back and forth—and I wasn't hurting! I was really throwing. I wasn't ready to go up against Nolan Ryan, but my arm felt different. It had some life to it.

Within a few days I began thinking that I should try throwing from the mound. I went to the bullpen and threw to a catcher for ten minutes. The next day I went for fifteen minutes and felt great.

Norm Sherry, our pitching coach, was watching. He suggested that I throw batting practice. The next day, June 19, I did. I was gaining momentum.

Atlee would sometimes stand behind the screen with the coaches, watching me throw. Other guys on the team would stop by and observe for a while. Robby Thompson, our second baseman, walked away shaking his head. "It's amazing," he said.

*   *   *

On Thursday, July 6, I had another MRI done and saw Dr. Muschler. He checked several lumps in my arm, including a large one that had filled in the gap where my tumor had been removed. Muschler told me this lump might be the tumor again, but it was too soon to tell. I didn't spend much time worrying about that. The coaches had scheduled a simulated game for me in St. Louis—my first taste of real pitching.

A simulated game is as close to a real game as you can make it. The hitters are from your own team, but they are trying to make you look bad, and you are trying to make *them* look bad. It's completely different from batting practice, where you just lay each pitch in there to be hit. It's a real test of your pitching ability.

I threw three innings, for a total of sixty pitches. I was able to put the ball where I wanted it most of the time. My fastball got up to eighty-two or eighty-three miles per hour, which was not bad. At my best it usually tops out at eighty-eight.

We returned home for the All-Star break, after which I pitched a second simulated game while the Pittsburgh Pirates were in town. I threw better and felt stronger. My fastball had a little more pop on it, and I began to get a few guys out.

I was then scheduled to throw a five-inning simulated game. The date was July 18, just over a month after Atlee had convinced me to take a chance and air it out. Now reporters were talking with me. Teammates were excited. Nobody could believe how far I had come. Not even me. I was moving full speed ahead.

Five innings meant that I would be throwing one hundred pitches. That's the same as a good, full-game effort. I was really fired up.

Dave Dravecky

The sun was warm on my shoulders, and rock music was blaring out over the field. I was hitting spots; I was throwing crisp pitches. And most of the time I was getting guys out.

Only one thing was missing. I was still a little tentative. It probably would not have been noticeable to anyone but another pitcher or a pitching coach. But they knew: I was still slightly afraid to let it go.

When I went out to pitch the last inning, Norm Sherry came over to me. "Dave," he said, "the last five or six pitches, just let it go. Air it out. Let's see what you can do."

So when the time came, I told the batter that I was going to let some fastballs rip. "Be careful," I said. I wasn't sure where they would head.

I wound up and let the ball go. *Boom!* Lo and behold, it went over the plate. More importantly, my arm did not pop off and roll toward first base. When I had thrown my one hundredth pitch Norm called a halt, and I jogged over to the screen.

"How fast was I?" I asked.

"You got up to eighty-five."

"Fantastic!" That was only three miles per hour less than my best. "I'm fired up now!"

I turned to Norm Sherry. "Hey, Norm, what do you think? I'm ready for some competition! I want to go down to Phoenix and get some guys out!"

9

Up Through the Minor Leagues

Five days later I drove to Stockton, California. The San Jose Giants—one of the Giants' minor league teams—were playing there, and I was the scheduled pitcher. I'd wanted to go to Phoenix, which is the Giants' top minor league team, but instead I'd been sent to try A-level ball, the lowest rung on the minor league ladder.

I had already heard over the radio that the game was sold out. Some of the San Francisco radio stations had announced that I'd be pitching. Still, I wasn't prepared for what I found at the stadium. Fans were lining up two hours before the game. The place buzzed with excitement.

I began to realize that this was more than an ordinary minor league baseball game. These fans hadn't come to yell at the umpire and cheer for home runs. Something deeper was involved. These fans had come because my comeback was touching their hearts. They were putting their hopes on me.

* * *

At game time, I took time to pray. I bowed my head in front of my locker and was quiet, putting the whole game before God. I told him that I trusted him with my life, and that I wanted to glorify him in whatever I did, win or lose.

Then I went out to the playing field, and the fans went nuts. It was a standing-room-only crowd. The stadium wasn't big, but it was bulging. There were extra people everywhere, pressing up against the fence, straining to see, making noise. This was my kind of baseball. I got excited.

While I was warming up, the lineups were announced. "And on the mound, making his first appearance of the 1989 season, number 43, Dave Dravecky!" The fans cheered loudly. By then I was extremely nervous. It was a minor league game, but I had major league jitters.

Our guys came up first. An outfielder named

Jim Cooper bunted his way on. Hustling all the way, he stole second, and the number three hitter singled him home. When I ran out to the pitcher's mound for my half of the inning, we were leading 1–0.

I toed the rubber and took a deep breath. I got the sign from my catcher, then wound up and threw. The batter swung and got a piece of it, fouling the ball back. Strike one. I threw again. Another foul, strike two. The third pitch he hit for a weak fly ball. The left fielder gathered it gently in, and I had my first out.

It felt great. This was something I knew how to do. And it was fun. Two ground-ball outs later I was in the dugout, kidding around with the guys.

People told me later they had never seen someone have so much fun playing baseball. It wasn't an act. I *was* having fun.

I went through the first three innings without giving up a hit. My fastball was crisp, mainly in the low eighties, but topping out at eighty-eight miles per hour. In the fourth inning I gave up my first hit, a single to left. That gave me a chance to use my pickoff move. My first throw over to first was a little off-target. I hadn't practiced the move at all and was rusty.

I looked in at my catcher, and he signaled for me to throw over to first again. I came to the set, looked at the runner—and when I made my throw, he was already headed for second, completely fooled. We cut him down. That got my juices flowing!

The fifth and sixth innings went quickly, except that I was beginning to feel tired. My pitches were coming up, which is always dangerous for me. I escaped any problems until the seventh—the final inning. Because we were playing the first part of a doubleheader, the game was shorter than usual.

The first batter I faced in the seventh smoked a double. I got the next man on a little fly ball, but by then my arm was weary and my control going fast. I walked the next hitter, putting the tying run on base—a terrible thing to do.

The sun was almost down. Deep green and golden colors painted the field. I took a deep breath, and delivered to the batter.

He was bunting on the first pitch, trying to move the runners into scoring position.

He squared and made a good bunt down the third base line—good in placement, but he had popped the ball into the air. My instincts kicked in. I took two quick, lunging steps and made an all-out, headlong dive for it, extending my mitt. I thought I could catch the ball before it hit the ground, and double off one of the runners. I got the ball—and watched it pop loose, out of my glove.

Getting to my knees, I grabbed the ball and pumped toward second. I saw that I would be late; the runner from first was already sliding. Danny Fernandez, my catcher, was beside me screaming, "Third, third!" I threw it there to force the runner, who had hesitated too long when I'd dived for the ball.

Out number two.

Boy, did I feel good. This was real baseball, and

I was a real pitcher, playing the only way I know how: all out, nothing held back. I'd gotten my uniform dirty.

I don't even remember how I got the last out. I just remember all the players gathering on the mound, slapping me and yelling as though we had won a play-off game. The crowd was yelling too.

When I search through my baseball memories, I don't find any game happier than that one. I was on top of the world.

*   *   *

I played my next game for the San Jose Giants in Reno, Nevada. Reno's stadium was old and battered. For this game, however, it was nearly full. Once again people had heard about my comeback from cancer and wanted to see for themselves.

I started without good control. Immediately I gave up some shots, and then a three-run home run. Some of the Reno players had been in Double-A baseball, and knew how to hit. It did not look good.

I made some adjustments, though, and settled down in the second and third innings, avoiding giving up more runs. My guys got some runs back, and we went into the lead.

Then in the fourth inning, as though the

floodlights had suddenly switched on, it happened. I locked in. Up until then, even in Stockton, I hadn't felt it. I'd been all right. But this was better than "all right." I felt I could hit a spot with my eyes closed. My breaking ball started snapping. For the last five innings I shut down the Reno team. I completed the game, throwing about one hundred pitches, and we won 7–3.

I came off the mound and told Duane Espy, the manager, "That's it, Duane. I'm ready for Phoenix."

He laughed and said, "Are you sure? I could use you around here for a few more games."

I called up Al Rosen, the Giants' general manager. He said I could move up to Phoenix, the highest level of the Giants' minor league system. If I did well there, the next step would be the major leagues.

* * *

Now that the end of my struggle was in sight, it was tempting to forget about living one day at a time. I wanted to get to the big leagues—badly. I could see it. I could taste it.

That is why, before the Friday game, I took time to pray. I didn't ask God for success. I asked that he either swing the door to the major leagues wide open, or slam it shut. I didn't want anything left unclear. My desire to succeed was so strong I thought I might push myself into a situation I wasn't really ready for, either physically or spiritually.

The way the game went, there was no doubt about which way the door was swinging. My pitching was the best yet. I didn't give up a run until the eighth inning. I didn't walk a soul. I got major leaguer Kevin Bass out. (He was in the minors like me, recuperating from an injury.) And I was locked in, with the old familiar feeling.

In the eighth inning I got rocked a bit, giving up two runs. In the dugout, the manager asked me whether I wanted to stay in the game. We were clinging to a one-run lead.

I didn't hesitate. "This baby's mine," I told him. "I'm closing. That's all there is to it, Bud. I'm going to win or lose this game."

I went out and shut them down. We won the game, 3–2. I had given up seven hits, struck out three, and walked none.

After the game I made a beeline into the clubhouse. I was looking for Bob Kennedy. He had come down from San Francisco just to see me pitch.

"Mr. Kennedy! Mr. Kennedy! Did you talk to Al Rosen?"

He walked over to me slowly, a little smile

Up Through the Minor Leagues   67

playing on his face. "Yes, I talked to him. I just got off the phone."

"What did he say? Don't you think I'm ready to go up to the big leagues?"

His voice grew softer. "Well, Dave, we think you probably had better stick around at this level for a little longer. If you can get a little more work, maybe a few more games. . . ."

I dropped to my knees. I knew he was messing

Dave Dravecky

with me. "Please, Mr. Kennedy, I'm ready. I want to go. Please send me to San Francisco."

He just looked down at me with that little smile.

"Pack your bags," he said. "Get out of here. Get your flight to San Francisco first thing tomorrow. You're going to the big leagues."

10

Starting Pitcher

We didn't realize how many other people were getting excited. To me and Janice, my return to the majors was a miracle—*our* miracle. We knew that some fans were interested—after all, four thousand people had shown up in Stockton—but we had no idea how many.

Not until Tuesday. By then Roger Craig had named me as Thursday's starter against the Cincinnati Reds. Every time I got into the car and turned on the radio, they were talking about me and the game. By Wednesday night I was *the* news in San Francisco.

The night before the game I told Janice there was no way I would sleep. I was just too excited.

Dave Dravecky

When my head hit the pillow, though, I must have been out in ten seconds. I slept so soundly Janice had to wake me up in the morning.

Before I left, we had a brief family prayer. All week we'd had tremendous commotion in the house, with guests and friends coming and going, but that morning we had a few quiet moments alone. We were upstairs in our bedroom, Janice and I sitting on the edge of the bed, Tiffany and Jonathan standing next to us. We all held hands and said some very simple words.

We prayed for my peace of mind. We really had no idea how the game would go. Even when I'd had all the muscles in my arm, on any given day I could go out to pitch and get shelled. So we prayed that whatever came, I'd have a sense of peace and calmness, and that I'd be able to glorify God through the way I performed. We didn't pray that I'd win—we never do that—but just that my attitude and my focus would be correct. And we gave thanks. We thanked God that he'd brought us to this point.

Janice began crying. In that quiet moment she suddenly realized what we were doing. Until then she'd been moving too fast.

Her tears upset Jonathan. "Mommy," he said, "what's wrong?"

Janice was too choked up to answer him.

He turned to me. "Daddy, why is Mommy crying?"

"Jonathan," I said, "those are tears of joy, not tears of sadness, because Daddy's going to pitch again. We never dreamed that this day would be possible. And here we are."

*　*　*

I felt almost eerily relaxed. My heart was full of thanks—thanks to God that I had the opportunity to pitch again, to do what I love so much. I was excited, but not worried. Win or lose, I was living a miracle. The doctors had told me that I would never pitch again, and today I was going to pitch.

Just before game time, Brett Butler and Bob Knepper, two of our veteran players, came over to my locker and said they'd like to pray. My close friend Scott Garrelts and Mackie Shilstone, the strength coach, joined us. They prayed for me for about ten minutes.

Then I went back to my locker and put on my white game uniform. "Giants" was blazoned across my chest, and "43" across my back.

Fifteen minutes before the game, I walked down the runway. Reaching the door that opens onto the field, I stepped into the glare of a brightly overcast day. For a second I was confused. In a

Dave Dravecky

long, ragged row photographers and TV cameramen were pointing their lenses at me. The cameras were whirring like a battery of machine guns. I looked at Norm, the pitching coach, who was standing by the door. "Holy smokes, Norm, what is going on?"

He just smiled. By then I probably could not have heard his answer, for the crowd had caught sight of me. The fans were yelling like crazy. I began taking off my jacket, and the cheering continued. It seemed to spread, up and out through the whole ballpark.

I just wanted to start throwing the ball, as quickly as possible. I strode to the bull pen mound. By the time I got there, the whole, huge stadium—34,810 fans—were on their feet, giving me a standing ovation.

Terry Kennedy was my catcher. He'd been my receiver when I broke into the major leagues, and he's a guy I like and respect tremendously. He also knows my pitching better than anyone. My heart was racing a hundred miles an hour. The noise was incredible. I looked at Terry and grabbed a bit of jersey over my heart, pounding it up and down to show him how my pulse was hammering. I pointed at him: "You too?" Terry looked back and, with a big smile, signaled that his heart was doing the same thing.

Then I began to throw, just playing catch with

Terry. As soon as I made the first toss, a sense of peace blanketed me. All I had to do now was what I know how to do best: throw a baseball.

I warmed up quickly, as I always do. When I was ready I walked down to the dugout. The cheers followed me. People were standing again. I could hear them yelling crazily in the stands, "Go get 'em, Dave!" "We're glad you're back, Dave!"

When it was time to play, I jogged out to the mound and heard the crowd noise swell to a roar. They were standing again, cheering for me. The scoreboard in center field flashed a gigantic, "WEL-COME BACK, DAVE."

I stood holding the ball, rubbing it, looking at Terry Kennedy. I jerked off my cap and waved it in acknowledgement of the cheering. I was suddenly overcome with emotion—with all the built-up emotion of the past ten months of struggle. I looked around me, up and up at the rows upon rows of cheering people. I have no words to describe my emotions. My heart was full.

I stepped off the mound to gather myself together. I thought, *Now is the time to say thank you, Lord. Just thanks. Thank you for the privilege of doing this again. Thank you that you restored my arm so I could pitch. But most of all, thank you for what you've done for me. Thank you for saving me.*

It didn't take long to do that, just a few

Dave Dravecky

moments. Then I stepped back up on the mound to start throwing. Immediately I was locked in. My rhythm and balance came effortlessly. From the first batter, Terry Kennedy and I were thinking together on pitch selection. It was like a picture: Terry and me playing catch, as though nobody else was around.

11

What a Day!

I am not a pitcher to blow people away with my blazing speed. I move the ball around, hit spots, catch batters leaning the wrong way, bust their bats with an inside pitch. I'm a pitcher who frustrates batters, because they're so sure they'll get me, until—what do you know!—they've gone 0 for 4.

The Cincinnati Reds did not give me the game out of sympathy. Even if they were touched by my comeback, we were in a pennant race. On August 10 we were in first place by two games, and the Reds wanted to beat us.

One of the sportswriters asked Pete Rose, the Cincinnati manager, whether he'd thought about the difficulty of what I was trying to do. Pete spit out a sunflower seed. "No," he said bluntly. "He's back, and it's great for him. I hope he loses."

The first hitter was Luis Quinones, the Reds' hustling second baseman. I started him off with a pitch high and outside, ball one. That set up the fastball inside. He turned on it, hard, and smashed the ball down the third-base line. But he had pulled it foul.

I thought he would be looking for that inside pitch again, so I went low and outside with my back-door slider, and picked up a strike. The count was one and two—much to my advantage. That's the way I like to pitch. Throw strikes, get ahead of the batter, and make every pitch a pitch of purpose.

The purpose of the next pitch was to get him swinging at a bad pitch. With two strikes he was vulnerable. But he laid off a slider outside.

I came back with the same pitch, only closer to the plate. I just missed the outside corner, and he took it for a ball. I think the call could have gone either way.

I now had a full count. I'd gone outside with three straight pitches. So I went there again. I thought he might still be thinking of that inside pitch he'd fouled off. I put my slider on the outside corner of the plate, just slicing a piece off the very edge. He had to dive down to get it, and all he could do was pop a fly ball into center field.

One out. The cheers rained down.

The second batter went quickly. I started him out with a fastball inside, and then came back with another which he grounded right at Matt Williams at third base.

Eric Davis was the third man in their lineup, one of the toughest hitters in baseball. I missed with my first two sliders outside. Behind in the count, I needed a strike. If in doubt about what to do, keep the ball down. I threw a sinking fastball over the plate. Davis hit the ball solidly, but on the ground. Matt Williams, with those wonderfully gentle hands of his, gobbled it up and threw across the diamond for an easy out.

As I ran in to the dugout, the crowd stood for another standing ovation.

That's how it went through seven innings. Every time I trotted in from the mound, the crowd stood to cheer.

Roger Craig said later that in all the decades he'd played and coached, he'd never seen so much emotion at a game. I had near-perfect control. Only four times did I go to three balls on a batter. I walked only one, toward the end of the game. And I entered the eighth inning having given up just one hit.

In the meantime, my guys were giving me the support I needed. We got a run in the second inning, then another in the third. The score became 4–0 in the fifth. Kevin Mitchell walked, and Matt

Williams crushed a first-pitch fastball into the left-field seats.

It turned out that I needed those runs.

* * *

In the seventh I began having some control problems. The ball began coming up. I didn't give up a hit, but I had to throw a lot of pitches.

What a Day!

Nobody particularly noticed. When you go into the eighth having given up only one hit, the manager is not thinking about pulling you.

I started off the eighth inning by breaking Todd Benzinger's bat. Unfortunately, the ball looped off his fists over second baseman Robby Thompson's head for a single. One of those little things again: a fluke hit, and most dangerously, a leadoff hit.

Their catcher was next. My first pitch to him was out over the plate, a pitch he might have hit a mile, but he didn't have a good swing at it. He hit a routine fly ball to left field. One out.

Their rookie third baseman, Scott Madison, came up next. I threw exactly the same pitch, and Madison killed it. It bounced off the wall in left, and he coasted in with a double.

With men at second and third and just one out, Pete Rose pinch hit Ron Oester. Oester gave me a tough at-bat. We battled to a three-and-two count. And then he swung and missed a back-door slider. The crowd roared. I pumped my fist.

Two outs. One more and I was out of trouble. Luis Quinones was up. The count went to two balls and one strike when I threw him my bread-and-butter pitch, a back-door slider. It wasn't a terrible pitch. It was up a little. It didn't break much. Quinones, who is no big slugger, turned on the ball and got all of his bat on it. The little white pill sailed high and deep to left, and I watched it with a sinking heart. It went over the chain-link fence in left field.

I felt sick. One bad pitch, and a four-run lead was reduced to one. It had happened so quickly that Roger didn't even have a relief pitcher warming up. I went ahead and pitched to their shortstop, who grounded weakly to short.

Going in to the dugout, I got another standing ovation.

*   *   *

I knew I was done. Sure enough, our manager pinch hit for me and called on Steve Bedrosian, our stopper, to pull the game out of the fire.

When Bedrosian went to the mound to warm up, the crowd started yelling. It took me a minute to realize that they were cheering for me. They wouldn't stop.

Terry Kennedy yelled, over the din, "Go on out there. It's your day. Take a bow." He nudged me. "C'mon, get going."

So I did. I went out on the field, looked up again at those rows upon rows of fans yelling their lungs out, and I lifted my cap. It was my twelfth standing ovation of the day.

I went back into the dugout, but the fans still wouldn't stop. They seemed to need to cheer, to pound their hands together and let out some emotion. They wanted me again. Some of the guys were gesturing at me. "Go out again! C'mon, Dave!" I walked up the steps. I looked up again at the thousands upon thousands of people whom I would never know, but who shared that moment with me. I lifted both my hands to the fans, in thanks.

*   *   *

Bedrosian was full of fire. He threw heat, and the heart of the Reds lineup couldn't handle it. Eric Davis grounded to short. Herm Winningham struck out. Ken Griffey struck out. Like that, the game was over.

I was on my feet before the last swinging strike. Terry Kennedy grabbed me for a hug. Other teammates were grabbing me, slapping me on the back, congratulating me on the game. Will Clark was one of the last to reach me. He opened his arms for a great big embrace. The fans still cheered, yelling as though they'd never stop, even as I walked off the field.

I got ice wrapped on my arm and went to the press conference. Everybody who was anybody in the world of news and entertainment was there. When I got up the room was quiet. I realized, almost as soon as I began answering questions, that I had something I needed to say.

"Before I take any more questions," I said, "it's important for me to give credit where credit is due. I want to give praise and glory to Jesus Christ for allowing me the opportunity to come back and play again." I went on to credit my doctors, my therapists, and my trainers, and all the others who had made it possible. But I tried to make clear that my comeback was a miracle for which God deserved the praise.

They asked me about my future. How did I feel? What about the rest of the baseball season? I told the reporters that I hoped to be able to pitch normally from that time on. "I feel great," I said.

12

Breaking Point

Then, suddenly, everything was normal. For the previous ten months I had lived with uncertainty. Would I come back? After that wonderful day of August 10, all doubt was gone. It felt oh, so good to go to the ballpark and work out as a regular team member.

On Monday we left for Montreal. For once, I was really excited to hit the road with the team. We got in late, and the next morning Bob Knepper and I headed out toward a bookstore Bob wanted to visit.

Walking along, we got talking about my experiences of the past week. I told Bob about how thankful I was. "Bob," I said, "you just have no idea how exciting it's been to live in the middle of a miracle. Then besides that, to get a chance to give the credit to Jesus Christ. Of everything I've done in baseball, that's the top."

Bob said, "Dave, it's great that you've had a chance to give God credit for your comeback. But I see another miracle. That's the miracle that God began in your life when you became a Christian eight years ago in Amarillo. It seems to me that's where we ought to place our focus. It's great that God's given you another chance to pitch. But that's pretty small, compared to the chance he's given you to live life with him eternally."

We continued to talk. I felt deeply excited and challenged. What, after all, did my comeback mean to people? What good did it do to encourage and inspire them to try harder, if they didn't even know why they were alive?

I couldn't see how I could get other people to see the bigger picture of God's love. But Bob's comments fit with my new sense of the amazing things God could do with my life. I wondered what God might do next.

* * *

Under the roof of Montreal's domed stadium that night there were perhaps 20,000 fans, a good crowd but nothing extraordinary. They gave me no standing ovation. I wasn't looking for one. I was looking for a chance to win my second game of the season. I was back to normal, and this was a normal game. That's the way I wanted it.

After three innings, I felt confident. I'd gone through their batting order without giving up a hit. When I came to bat, I got a hit myself. I wasn't throwing quite as hard as I had five days before, and my control wasn't as sharp, but I was moving the ball around, keeping it down, and making the adjustments that were necessary to win.

In the fifth inning I struggled with my control, but Roger Craig wasn't thinking about warming up a relief pitcher. He thought I was cruising along.

In the dugout after the fifth, I rubbed my left arm. It felt strange. It didn't hurt, exactly; it just tingled.

Brett Butler, our center fielder, was standing near me. He noticed what I was doing and came over. "Is everything all right?" he asked.

"Yeah, everything's fine," I said. "I just feel a little stiffness." The tingling felt as though it came from my muscles.

Long ago, Dr. Muschler had warned me that if I ever felt any pain in my arm I should quit throwing immediately or I might break my arm. But I wasn't thinking about that. I'd done so much in the months since those warnings, and I'd never had the

Dave Dravecky

slightest problem. I never thought this might be a warning sign.

We made a little excitement that inning. Will Clark singled, and with one out Matt Williams tagged one deep. That made the score 3–0 when I jogged out to the mound for the bottom of the sixth. The heart of the Expos lineup was coming up.

I started wrong, coming out over the plate to Damaso Garcia and watching the ball fly over the left-field fence for a home run. Andres Gallaraga was next up. I came inside, just as he was diving out over the plate expecting an outside pitch. I'd fooled him, but the pitch was too far inside. It nicked him. He went down to first base.

Robby Thompson came over from second. "You feeling okay?" he asked.

"I feel great!"

Three thousand miles away in California, Janice was sitting by the pool at our condominium complex, talking with my mom and dad and watching Tiffany and Jonathan swim. The game wasn't on TV, so she was listening on her little portable radio. When I hit Gallaraga she got nervous. She began talking to our manager, Roger Craig. "Get him out of there, Roger," she said. "Take him out before he gets into trouble." Roger wasn't listening.

Tim Raines came up. I had the ball in my glove, and I rubbed it thoroughly. I was unhappy about putting a runner on base, and I knew I would have to bear down to get Raines out. He's a very tough hitter, and he represented the tying run.

I came to the set position, stared over at Gallaraga at first, then pivoted on my left leg, at the same moment pulling my left hand up and back for the pitch. Pushing off the rubber, I threw.

Next to my ear I heard a loud popping noise. The sound could be heard all over the field. It sounded as though someone had snapped a heavy tree branch.

I felt as though my arm had broken off from my body and was sailing toward home plate. I grabbed at my arm, trying to pull it back. The ball left my hand and flew high up, past an astonished Terry Kennedy, who went charging after it.

But I knew nothing about the ball, or about the runner who ran hesitantly around the bases, as though, for once, he was truly guilty of stealing. I was grabbing my arm to keep it from flying away, and tumbling headfirst down the mound. I shouted with all the air in my lungs. Over I went, doing a complete 360 degree tumble, then flopping forward until I came to rest on my back, my feet pointing toward center field. I have never felt such pain.

In an instant Will Clark was there, looking down at me. I was writhing and grunting, trying to get my breath. "Oh, Will, it hurts, it's killing me! It's broke. It's broke. It feels like I've broken my arm."

Dave Dravecky

13

Changing My Focus

Even through the pain, my thoughts flowed clearly. When I hit the ground I thought that the bone had broken through my skin. It must be sticking out of my shoulder, I thought. I didn't want to touch it, but I had to find out. Carefully working my right hand up my arm, I found that everything was together.

Meanwhile I was shaking and grunting and crying out from the pain. Above and around me, the stadium was awesomely silent.

The pain gradually grew weaker until I could lie quietly, looking up at the circle of faces. Roger

Craig, feeling helpless, leaned down and hugged me.

I was simply amazed at what was going on. I'd thought the book had been written on my comeback, and I could go back to normal. Now this. I wasn't, not even for a split second, angry. I was simply astonished, and full of the certainty that God was writing another chapter in my life. Something more, something amazing, was being revealed.

They brought a stretcher and wanted to get me on it. I said no. "Let me walk off," I said between gritted teeth. "I'm all right."

"Shut up, Dave. You're not walking."

I finally managed to struggle onto the stretcher. They wheeled me off, through the tunnel and into the training room.

In the clubhouse, a doctor wrapped my arm tightly against my body. A handful of players and coaches were watching. Ballplayers are not big on showing emotion—especially not tender emotions. That day, though, emotions ran out of control. Terry Kennedy expressed the feelings when he told a reporter, "I've known Dave a long time, and he's probably as good a friend as I've got. This is not supposed to happen to people like him. This is not supposed to happen to good people."

After the game, Roger Craig was completely unable to speak. He broke into tears in front of reporters, who had to wait in embarrassed silence for a solid minute before he could talk.

The game continued while I lay in the training room. Suddenly Mike Fitzgerald, the Expos' catcher, came running in with all his catcher's gear on. Mike looked at me with tears in his eyes, grabbed me by the back of my head, and pulled me next to him. He hugged me and kissed me. "I love you, brother," he said, and turned and went running out. I just watched him go in amazement. I'm fairly sure that had never happened in baseball before.

An ambulance arrived, and they were about to wheel me away when Bob Knepper put his head near mine and suggested that we pray.

I don't remember what Bob said. It wasn't what he said, though, so much as how he said it. Bob had a hard time getting his words out. His voice was cracking. Love for me filled his prayer.

While he prayed, the inning ended, and Giants' players came racing in from the playing field to find out how I was. We could hear them running toward us, and then, as they entered the room, falling silent. By the time Bob finished, the room was jammed with twenty-five guys, all dead silent. Overwhelming emotion filled the air. I looked up and saw that many of my teammates had tears in their eyes.

For me, Bob's prayer took away any remaining anxiety. I knew I was in God's hands.

Dave Dravecky

As I was being wheeled out, I turned to Terry Kennedy. He was standing next to me, his eyes full of tears, staring as if to say, *What on earth is going to happen to you next?*

"Hey," I said, "if there was ever anything to the saying 'Win one for me,' this is it, guys. I don't want that lead to disappear, because I'm probably not going to pitch again this season, and I want my record to be 2–0. I want to end the year undefeated."

Terry looked at me as though I had lost my mind.

Then I greeted the ambulance driver. "This has been kind of a rough day," I told him, "so please get me there safely. I've had enough excitement already."

*   *   *

After the doctors put on a cast, they saw no reason to keep me at the hospital. Shortly before midnight, I headed back to my room in a taxi. My frame of mind was almost bizarre, it was so positive. I certainly didn't enjoy breaking my arm, nor would I care to ever repeat that tumbling-down-the-mound trick. But emotionally I was still riding the excitement that had begun on August 10, and had been kicked up a notch by my talk with Bob Knepper. I had no idea what was going to come next in this adventure, but I trusted that God had good things in store for me.

When I got back to the hotel room, still in my uniform, I called Janice. I wanted her to hear from me that I was all right.

Scott Garrelts was there, and so was Jeff Brantley, who had come in to relieve me when I'd broken my arm. I'd heard at the hospital that we'd won the game. While I was talking to Janice, I saw Steve Bedrosian out in the hallway. He had come on in the ninth to preserve my game once again; we'd won by another one-run score, 3–2.

"Hey, Bedrock! Bedrock! Way to go! Thanks for saving the game, man! Now I'm 2–0, and I've got some negotiating power for next year!"

I was feeling pretty rowdy for someone who's just broken his arm. Janice said it sounded like a party was going on.

Pretty soon it settled down to me, Scott Garrelts, Jeff Brantley, Greg Litton, and Bob Knepper. We raided the mini-bar in the room, drinking up all the Cokes and eating all the chocolate bars. I was starting to feel really hungry, so we sent Jeff and Scott out for some fast food. They were gone for about an hour, and came in soaking wet and carrying a ton of junk food. They'd been running all over Montreal in the rain, trying to find a hamburger place.

Dave Dravecky

By then it was probably 2:00 A.M. I knew it was going to be tough for me to rest, since the doctors had told me to sleep sitting up.

"Hey, why don't we just stay up all night?" I suggested.

We stayed awake until 5:00 A.M., talking about every subject under the moon. When there was light leaking over the horizon, we closed our time together with prayer, and the others disappeared to catch some sleep. I felt a wonderful sense of peace. I took some aspirin and dozed for two and a half hours before it was time to get up again.

* * *

On August 10, I had thought that media attention had reached an absolute peak. I soon found there was another level. On August 15 all the late news programs began their coverage with the horrifying film of my arm breaking. Soon every major network wanted a special interview. Dozens of magazines and newspapers were calling. So was Hollywood, to talk about motion pictures.

With my arm breaking, the focus shifted. The press had written about my comeback as a miracle, but what could they call this? The opposite of a miracle? If coming back from cancer had lifted people's hopes, should this dash them? That wasn't how I saw it. I saw my life as one long adventure in partnership with God. The miracle of my life had begun in Amarillo, and it continued.

I told the reporters that I hoped to be able to come back and pitch again. I had no intention of quitting. But that wasn't the basic source of my optimism. My optimism was grounded in Jesus Christ. When you've done everything you can, and yet everything seems to have fallen apart, you need to know that God can overcome.

Before, the press had told the world about my physical recovery. Now they reported on my positive attitude, as if that were a bigger miracle. In a way, it was.

14

The Play-offs

When the doctors in San Francisco finished examining me, they had good news. The break in my arm was just an ordinary kind. My bone must have been weak, still recovering from being frozen, and the stress of pitching had opened a hairline crack. That's what had caused the tingling. If I had remembered Dr. Muschler's warning, if I had stopped and taken myself out of the game, I could have been pitching again in the postseason.

Even so, the future didn't look too bad. Nobody before me had pitched after losing his deltoid muscle, but plenty of people had pitched after breaking an arm. Dr. Campbell saw no reason why I couldn't return for the 1990 season.

However, the weeks around the 1989 play-offs were extremely difficult for me. First off, I couldn't get a decent night's sleep. Because of my arm, I wasn't allowed to sleep lying down. Night after night I tossed and turned. Day after day I grew more tired.

Also, Janice had to bathe me. I just don't like the feeling of helplessness. And I was frustrated that I couldn't play. I would go to the ballpark and try to be a good cheerleader, but soon I felt like an invisible man. I had never had to sit in the dugout and watch my team play for a championship.

The first two games of the National League play-offs were in Chicago's Wrigley Field. In the first game, Will Clark clubbed two home runs, and we won 11–3. Everybody was happy but me. That night I didn't sleep. I ached. It wasn't just my arm that ached, either. It was my whole body, aching to be in the game.

If you only looked at the final scores of the 1989 National League Championships you might think they were lacking in drama. In reality, they were tight, exciting games.

We came to the fifth game leading three games to one. We were determined to win so we wouldn't have to go back to Wrigley Field. It was Mike Bielecki pitching for the Cubs against our Rick Reuschel. The Cubs had eaten Rick for breakfast in the second game of the series, but today he had them crossed up in every direction. And Mike

Dave Dravecky

Bielecki was locked in. None of us could figure out his pattern.

We came to the bottom of the eighth inning tied at one run apiece. Bielecki had pitched almost flawlessly, giving up only three hits—one a triple to Will Clark that had allowed us to tie the game. With two outs, Roger Craig sent in Candy Maldonado to hit for Reuschel.

I'd talked to Candy before the game. While everyone else was laughing and kidding around, he had been scrunched down in front of his locker, looking miserable. Roger wasn't starting him, and he hated to sit on the bench.

Over the All-Star break, while he was home in Puerto Rico, Candy had committed himself to follow Christ. For as long as I could remember, Candy had flirted with Christianity, but he hadn't wanted to give up his lifestyle. Over the break, though, he'd finally come to a decision.

For the first two weeks after that, he'd hit the ball all over the lot. He thought it was because he'd found God. Those of us who were Christians hadn't wanted to discourage him, but we'd warned him that it didn't work that way.

And sure enough, Candy slumped to his worst year ever in the major leagues. I have to hand it to him, though: he hung in there. He didn't quit the faith, and he didn't quit trying to play.

When I saw him in the clubhouse he looked at

me with his big brown eyes full of pain and said, "Dave, I know how I'm supposed to act on the outside. I'm know I'm supposed to keep my feelings under control. But inside I am hurting so bad. Inside I am so. . . ." He broke it off. He couldn't talk.

I was feeling some similar feelings. It was so hard not to play. "Candy," I said, "I know you can't just push it aside. I know it hurts, and that's the way it has to be. But keep your focus on the Lord, and when you get an opportunity, you'll be ready."

When Candy was sent in to pinch hit, I began to pray for him. By then I was out in front of the bench, crouched down, screaming through every pitch. I told God, "I know you don't want me to pray like this, but I'm going to anyway, because this guy has been in a pit and I want him to succeed." I prayed that Candy would hit a home run and be a hero. All through his at-bat I prayed for him.

Candy didn't hit a home run. He did something more unusual: he showed patience. He kept fouling off pitches, fouling off pitches, working Bielecki deeper into the count. Finally he took a walk.

A little thing. A walk, with nobody on base, with two outs.

Bielecki lost his game plan. He said later that he was tired, but you really should be able to throw strikes even when you are tired. Candy had pushed him to the limits and drawn a walk, and now, with 62,000 fans on their feet and their screams bouncing off the concrete bleachers, each strike became harder to find. He's a young pitcher, and I'm sure his heart was hammering. I know mine would have been. He walked Brett Butler. Then he walked Robby Thompson. Bases loaded. And that set the stage for Will Clark.

There is nobody I would rather have at the plate when crunch time comes. When the game is on the line, Will's round, dark, glittering eyes seem to stare through you. All he sees is the baseball.

The Cubs' manager, Don Zimmer, brought in Mitch Williams to pitch. It was the perfect matchup: youth vs. youth, lefty vs. lefty, strength vs. strength, our best vs. their best. Williams's nickname is Wild Thing.

I thought Mitch would walk home a run. But his first pitch was a strike. I knew then it was going to be a battle. Wild Thing was throwing heat.

I also saw something in Will. He was staying in. Sometimes he, like all lefties facing another lefty, tends to bail out. After all, the ball comes in like it's heading straight for your head. It's natural to duck, especially with Mitch Williams throwing wild stuff that could literally kill you. But Will wasn't flinching.

On the second pitch, a fastball, he swung but fouled it weakly away. He took a ball, then fouled off a slider. He foul-tipped a fastball high in the strike zone, just staying alive. He took a fastball away, evening the count at 2–2. Then Mitch threw a fastball high in the zone again, a pitch that Will often misses, and Will swung, locking his hips and connecting with that sweet, smooth swing, and the ball darted cleanly over second base and into center field. Two runs came home, and the air of Candlestick was thick with sound.

After we went ahead 3−1, I walked back to the clubhouse to put the brace on my arm. I wanted to celebrate, and I wanted to avoid hurting my arm while I did it. I couldn't believe it: my second World Series in five years.

The game was not over, however. The Cubs began the top of the ninth like batting practice, zinging hard line drives in every direction. A run came home, and the stands fell silent. There were two men on and two outs when Ryne Sandberg, Chicago's great second baseman, came to the plate. Sandberg is a pure fastball hitter. Steve Bedrosian was throwing nothing but fastballs and getting tagged.

Terry Kennedy went out to talk to Steve. He told him to go with his slider, since the fastball wasn't working.

Bedrosian's slider hadn't been effective lately, but he threw one, down and away. Sandberg swung and hit a soft ground ball to Robby Thompson at second. Robby wheeled and threw to first. It was over. We were on our way to the World Series.

Everybody rushed out of the dugout, toward

the mound, jumping on top of Bedrosian and Clark, piling together. I followed cautiously, wanting to be careful of my arm, but wanting to join the celebration. I never thought about being hit from behind. Someone—I have no idea who—slammed into me. I was thrown into the pile, and astounding pain blazed through my arm. It hurt as much as it had in Montreal.

I went down into a crouch, holding the arm

against my body, trying to protect it from the surging, leaping pile of bodies around me. Then Dusty Baker, our hitting coach, saw me and came to help. He and our trainer, Mark Letendre, pulled me out and led me off the field, holding my arm in pain while the rest of the team continued to celebrate.

15

What More Can Happen?

My arm hurt more after this break than it had after Montreal. I couldn't sleep. I couldn't bathe myself. I couldn't get a coat on. I couldn't cut my meat. Janice had to do everything for me, and when she forgot, I would stand there like a hurt puppy until she noticed. I hate to ask for help.

The World Series began five days later, in Oakland. We weren't in awe of the Athletics, but we had played them eleven times in spring training and lost ten. That had been spring, of course, when nothing counts, but still we remembered.

We lost two games in Oakland that weren't

even close—the scores were 5–0 and 5–1—and we came back to Candlestick Park knowing we had a very big mountain to climb. The weather had continued unnaturally warm. Ordinarily you wear a coat to Candlestick. But now in mid-October, it was t-shirt weather.

I was sitting in front of my locker, talking to Bob Knepper, when it happened. We felt a low rumble in the floor, like an airplane passing overhead. We stopped talking and looked at each other.

"That feels like an earthquake," Bob said.

"It *is* an earthquake," I said.

The room was shaking. Players ran out the door of the clubhouse, toward the parking lot. In seconds Bob and I joined them.

By the time we stopped in the open area just outside the stadium, the shaking had stopped. People all around were talking loudly, laughing and shaking their heads. Soon, reporters came asking for reactions. They said that the Bay Bridge was down, that a wall had collapsed in San Francisco. I began to realize that something serious had happened.

We had a full house that night. Friends and relations staying in nearby hotels had no electricity, and we invited them over. Listening to the news of our neighbors all around the Bay, and of all the people who had died, we felt thankful for our lives.

Dave Dravecky

Nevertheless, Janice and I went to bed that night wondering what more could happen to us.

A week after the earthquake, Janice, Tiffany, Jonathan, and I left for home in Ohio. My arm was still killing me. I had reached such a low point emotionally that I didn't even care about the final games of the World Series, which had been delayed by the earthquake. Two days later, I drove up to the Cleveland Clinic for a routine check on my arm. I went up alone and did my time in the MRI cylinder.

The next day, Janice and I met Dr. Bergfeld. He wasn't jolly. He spoke very soberly and slowly, sometimes looking down at the ground. Both breaks, he said, seemed to be healing well. He mentioned a pitcher who had broken his arm twice, yet come back to play again. But then Dr. Bergfeld stopped and put his head down. "I'm not even concerned about that right now. I'm concerned about the lump. We really need to talk about these MRI results."

That was when the conversation really grew serious. He had no way to be sure, but he said that the new lump on my arm looked exactly like a desmoid tumor. He thought that the tumor had come back.

*   *   *

"Did you understand what the doctors were saying?" Janice asked when we were in the car together, driving home. "David, do you realize that they didn't mention your future in baseball, even once?"

I didn't respond right away, because I didn't want to think about it. All my life, I'd set my face toward playing baseball, pushing on no matter what the odds might be against me. That was the only way I knew to think.

"Yeah," I said finally. "It's real sobering."

"David," Janice said. "David, what are you going to do?"

"There you go again," I said, trying to joke. "Writing me off."

"David, what would you say to me if I were in your shoes? If I had cancer and I wanted to keep on with my career no matter what the risk, what would you say?"

That was easy. "I'd tell you to quit. Immediately. But Janice, you can't tell me what to do. I have to make this decision for myself."

Janice really got mad with me then. She said it made her sick to think of me going out there and taking those risks. "Enough is enough," she said. "After what we've been through in the last year, why would you do it? Would you risk your arm to throw that ball again? Is baseball that important?"

I didn't answer. I just knew that I wanted to

keep playing. It was an instinct. No matter what, you keep on. That had been my motto; I'd even tacked it up in my locker, where I could look at it each day: "Never give up."

I called up Atlee the next day. I expected him to tell me to keep on—or at least to see how my arm felt in spring training. He was somber when he heard about the tumor, however. I described Janice's question—"What would you say if I were in your shoes?"

"If my wife had a tumor," he said, "I know exactly what I'd say. I'd tell her to quit."

How do you quit, though? How do you leave something you love, something that has been your life?

*   *   *

As I thought about the possibility of quitting, as I let that idea take root in my mind, I was surprised to find that it brought me peace. That threw me a little.

What would I gain, driving myself and my family through another comeback? What could I get from baseball that I hadn't already received? Why not quit? It came down to this: I would miss the game. And I would miss my friends.

A week after coming home to Ohio, Janice and

What More Can Happen?   109

I traveled back to California again. Long before, we had committed ourselves to several speaking engagements.

On Friday I saw Atlee. I told him that I had made the decision to retire from baseball.

He was thoughtful. "It's interesting," he said. "Bob Knepper called me yesterday, and we talked about you. Bob told me he was praying that you would have peace about retiring from baseball.

"I couldn't pray that way for you," Atlee said. "I didn't know what you ought to do. I've just been praying that you would be at peace in whatever God led you to decide."

"I am, Atlee," I said. "It's as though a tremendous pressure has been released."

When we got back to his house, Atlee asked Janice if she was happy about the decision. I could see her struggle with her answer. She was happy, yes—happy that I would be home, happy that we could work on the tumor without trying to think about a future in baseball as well. But for all of us— Janice and me, Atlee and his wife, Jenny—the full meaning of retirement began to hit. There would be no more baseball together.

We'd spent so many hours together. We'd been so close. I'd gone through the batting order with Atlee each game, discussing how to pitch to every last guy in the National League. Atlee had been the guy who would call me fifteen minutes

after he'd dropped me off—calling me because he
had thought of one last thing he had to say.

That night, after we'd said good-bye to Atlee
and Jenny, after Janice and I had climbed into our
hotel bed and pulled the covers up, I lay in the
darkness thinking.

"What am I going to do about Atlee?" I said to
Janice. "My buddy Atlee, what am I going to do?"

16

An End and a Beginning

Right from the beginning, my doctors had warned me that a desmoid tumor is a pest, hard to get rid of. If a single cell is left, the tumor will grow back. That's exactly what happened. My broken arm didn't knock me out of baseball. The tumor did. It kept coming back.

On January 4, I went to the Sloan Kettering hospital in New York City for a second operation. A new doctor, Murray Brennan, cut away the cancer and sewed some thin plastic tubes inside my arm. A week later he put pellets of radioactive iridium into those tubes. Radioactive material was right inside my arm where the tumor had been. It was supposed to kill any cancer cells that remained.

My doctors expressed tremendous hope that they would get rid of my tumor this time. I took their word for it, but somehow, in the back of my mind, I wasn't so sure. My slogan stayed the same: prepare for the worst, hope for the best.

As it turned out, that operation was the beginning of a long, dark year and a half. First my arm wouldn't heal from the surgery. The scar stayed red and raw, and a little hole developed in it. Gradually the hole grew bigger, so big you could put your finger inside my arm and tap the bone. My son, Jonathan, thought that was a neat trick.

Because of that hole, I went back for another operation in May. This time I was in the hospital for twelve days. The doctor took a muscle out of my back and wrapped it around the bone in my arm.

While he was operating, however, the doctor made a troubling discovery: the tumor had come back again. It was growing near my radial nerve, which is extremely important for controlling your hand. I'd noticed my hand feeling numb, and tingling as if from an electric shock. Apparently this was the reason.

Dr. Brennan still felt optimistic. I started another type of radiation treatment. I got that treatment in Cleveland during July and August, driving to the hospital five days a week.

An End and a Beginning 113

When I finally got done with that treatment, I was sick of the hospital. For a whole year I'd been dragging my arm in and out of treatment, and I wanted to get on with my life. But just when I was feeling hopeful about my arm, I came down with a fever and the doctor slapped me in the hospital again. He said I had a staph infection in my arm, and it was serious.

I was really sick of being sick. I felt as if I'd been in a boxing ring with a lightweight punching me, and just about the time I was exhausted they put in a heavyweight. Every time I turned around something new hit me in the face.

Even after I got out of the hospital I had nurses coming to my house twice a day to give me antibiotics through a tube. I felt sick to my stomach a lot of the time. The infection would get better, and then my fever would flare up, I'd start to feel nauseous, and the whole cycle would start again.

The worst was this: my arm wasn't getting better. The hole wouldn't heal up. My fingers felt numb, and I could hardly move my arm. Deep down inside I began to doubt that my arm was ever going to get well.

In May of 1991 I went to New York for my regular three-month exam. Dr. Brennan examined me solemnly, and then he looked at me. "I really do think it's time," he said. I knew instantly what he was talking about. It was time to cut off my arm.

In a way I was relieved to hear it. I wanted to go ahead with my life, and my arm had become a nuisance to me. It just wasn't getting any better. So I wasn't shocked by what Dr. Brennan said. I simply replied, "Okay. When do you want to do it?"

That's why I woke up one day in early June without a left arm or shoulder. I hadn't known for sure that I would lose the arm when I'd gone under the anesthesia. But when Dr. Brennan opened up my arm, he found the same old bad news. The tumor had come back for the third time. Dr. Brennan took my shoulder as well as my arm to make sure that the tumor would never return.

When I woke up Janice and my mom were at the foot of my bed, looking at me full of love and concern. The doctors and nurses had worried that I might go into shock from the operation, but they soon saw I was fine. In fact, I felt better. During the six days I was in the hospital I walked a mile a day.

So many people had sent me flowers and candy there wasn't room for them in my room, so I shared the wealth with other patients on the floor. We had a great time, almost a party. I had prayed that God would use Janice and me in a special way while we were at the hospital, and God answered that prayer. A lot of the other patients were much sicker than I ever had been. I was able to see beyond my own situation and respond to people around me who were hurting.

An End and a Beginning

17

Was It Worth It?

Just a short time ago I was a major league baseball player. I could do things with a baseball that few people in the world can do. Now, it's hard to put toothpaste on my toothbrush. It's hard to cut my meat. I'm struggling to do what most people do with ease.

You don't realize how many times you need both hands until you have only one. I like to challenge people: just try to put your pants on with one hand. I guarantee you will have more sympathy for amputees if you do. I'm getting pretty good at it, but sometimes I go to put my left leg in the pant leg and I miss. Then I fall straight over like a redwood tree, with a very loud crash.

Of course, I'm learning how to manage. Already I've learned how to write with my right hand, and I can manage a pretty good signature. I can even write a letter. The trouble is, everything is slow. I have to take time. I've never been a patient person, and I find it very hard to learn that virtue now.

I've also been troubled by pain—not pain from the operation, but a weird kind of pain that began after I got out of the hospital. The doctors call it "phantom pain." That's because it comes from a phantom—the arm that's no longer there. It's fairly common among amputees. Apparently the nerves that were cut when my arm was amputated keep sending signals to my brain. For weeks I felt like my hand was on fire. Now the pain has decreased, but it still hurts, especially when I think about it.

I can "feel" my arm. It's in a bent position, and it feels as though I have a cast on it. When I "flex" my muscle—the muscle that isn't there—I can feel the whole arm. Most of the time, though, I sense my hand. It's cramping, all day long, and then suddenly something like an electric shock goes through it and I can feel my hand open up.

The way I look at it, I lived with a lot of pain as a pitcher. Often my arm was hurting, and I just pitched through the pain. If I lived with that, I can live with this. I'm told the pain may go away in time, but there's no guarantee.

The hardest part, though, isn't the pain, and it's

not the slowness. It's the loss. I've lost something that meant a very great deal to me. All my life I've been a baseball player. My left arm made me one. Now it's gone. I won't be able to swing a bat ever again. I can't throw a fastball by a hitter. The dream I had from the time I was a little boy is over.

At first I didn't have time to think about that. When I'd look at myself in the mirror, I wouldn't take time to really look, I'd just walk away. I was trying to pretend that it didn't matter. Then one day I couldn't pretend anymore.

I was lying on my bed, feeling really frustrated with my life, and all my feelings built up until I couldn't contain them. I said to myself, "I'm sick of it. I'm tired of being an amputee." I lay there for a long time thinking about how bad I felt. I wanted to cry. That was the first time I'd taken time to miss my arm, to realize that it was gone for good, to let that sadness sink in.

I lay there and let my mind go back to my days in Little League, in high school and college, in the minors and the majors. I recalled fond memories of throwing the ball, getting people out. I would never get to do that again.

But after feeling wretched for a while, I began to realize something else: Nothing could take those memories from me. They were mine forever. Meanwhile, I thought, life goes on. I can't play professional baseball any more, but I can be a

118   Dave Dravecky

husband to my wife and a dad to my kids. It's time to move on to new challenges.

I think I'll always be an athlete at heart. I've made up my mind to try to do whatever my heart desires. If I can't do it, I'll find out through the process of trying. So far, I've found I can do quite a lot. I enjoy fishing, although I can't bait my hook. I enjoy playing catch with Jonathan. I enjoy playing football. I lift weights to keep in shape.

I've done quite a bit of swimming, and some people swear I swim faster with one arm than they do with two. When I first began swimming I wondered if I would just go in a circle, but that's not a problem. I'm not as fast as I'd like to be, but I still have fun and get my exercise.

The same for playing golf. I've always enjoyed the game, and now I'm getting to work at it. It's been nice to play a game without the pressure of being expected to be the best.

I know it's sometimes hard for people to look at me without an arm. When people see someone with a handicap, they feel strange, and they don't know what to say. I know they do, because that's how I felt. Let me tell you: I'm just exactly the same Dave Dravecky I always have been. So if you see me or anyone with a handicap, don't worry about saying the wrong thing or hurting their feelings. Treat them like a normal person—because you know what? That's exactly what we are.

* * *

The end of this story is bittersweet, of course. I came back, but only for a short time. Some people have asked whether it was worth struggling for that whole year in order to pitch only twice at the major league level. Was it worth it, considering how it ended?

I don't even have to hesitate. Yes, it was worth it. It was an unforgettable thrill. When I think of my years in baseball I put those games in Stockton, San Francisco, and Montreal at the very top.

I got to live out the greatest boyhood dream of all. I got to do what the experts said was impossible, to come back from cancer and pitch a major league baseball game. Without a deltoid muscle in my pitching arm, I won a game in a pennant drive in front of tens of thousands of screaming fans. What more would anybody want out of baseball? The fans who supported me, screamed for me, prayed for me, wrote to me—they knew that it was worth it.

We all know that baseball isn't going to last forever. But while my baseball career did last, I got to experience one incredible year. I gained some wonderful memories I'll treasure forever. And I believe I gave other people some pretty good memories too.

The struggle was also worth it because of the growth it brought in my life. I've learned a lot. I've learned how precious my wife and my children are. They were always important, but never so precious to me as they are now.

I've learned to value serving other people. Because of what I've been through, I've had opportunities to talk to many, many people and offer them encouragement and the grace of God. As much as I love baseball, I treasure that more.

Perhaps most of all, I've learned to put my life in God's hands. At times, the uncertainty of the last four years almost drove me wild. I had to learn to do what was within my grasp, one day at a time, and leave the rest to God.

Such are the lessons that come when a man faces adversity. I don't think I could have gained them in any other way. If you don't struggle, you don't grow.

When I think back on my career in baseball, I can't help but smile. I feel some sadness, but more satisfaction. How could I feel anything else?

Every year in America hundreds of thousands of kids go out to play Little League, and every year they dream of playing in the major leagues. The odds are so slim. It's as if you had a huge stadium jammed full of kids, each wearing a uniform and a glove, and just one out of all those thousands gets picked to come down onto the field and play with the big boys.

I was that kid. I got to play.

And even more: I got the chance to come back.

If you would like to write to Dave Dravecky, you can reach him at:

The Dave Dravecky Foundation
P.O. Box 3505
Boardman, OH 44513